Promises
of
Encourage-
ment

W9-ABD-678

Harold Shaw Publishers
Wheaton, Illinois

Grateful acknowledgment is made to the publishers of the Scripture versions, portions of which are quoted in this book, using the following abbreviations:

NASB   New American Standard
NIV   New International Version
NKJ   New King James
TLB   The Living Bible

Portions from:

THE NEW AMERICAN STANDARD BIBLE, copyright 1960, 1962, 1963, 1968, 1971, 1972, 1973, 1975, 1977 by the Lockman Foundation. Used by permission.

THE NEW INTERNATIONAL VERSION, © 1973, 1978, 1984 by the International Bible Society. Used by permission.

THE NEW KING JAMES VERSION, copyright © 1979, 1980, 1982, Thomas Nelson Inc., Publishers.

THE LIVING BIBLE, © 1971 by Tyndale House Publishers, Wheaton, Illinois. Used by permission.

ISBN 0-87788-650-4

Cover photo © H. Abernathy/H. Armstrong Roberts

99 98 97 96 95

10 9 8 7 6 5 4

I waited patiently for God to help me; then he listened and heard my cry. He lifted me out of the pit of despair, out from the bog and the mire, and set my feet on a hard, firm path and steadied me as I walked along. He has given me a new song to sing, of praises to our God. Now many will hear of the glorious things he did for me, and stand in awe before the LORD, and put their trust in him.

Psalm 40:1-3, *TLB*

Contents

Introduction

Our heavenly Father's nature is one of compassion and mercy. The apostle Paul describes him as "the Father of compassion and the God of all comfort" (2 Corinthians 1:3, *NIV*).

The Bible is full of God's promises to comfort, encourage, and sustain those who suffer. This book gathers together many of these promises to strengthen you and to give you a firm and joyful hope.

God Is the Source of Compassion

"God washes the eyes by tears until they can behold the invisible land where tears shall come no more."

HENRY WARD BEECHER

Praise be to the God and Father of our Lord Jesus Christ, the Father of compassion and the God of all comfort, who comforts us in all our troubles, so that we can comfort those in any trouble with the comfort we ourselves have received from God. *2 Corinthians 1:3-4, NIV*

Yet the LORD longs to be gracious to you; he rises to show you compassion. For the LORD is a God of justice. Blessed are all who wait for him! *Isaiah 30:18, NIV*

They will neither hunger nor thirst, nor will the desert heat or the sun beat upon them. He who has compassion on them will guide them and lead them beside springs of water. *Isaiah 49:10, NIV*

As a mother comforts her child, so will I comfort you; and you will be comforted over Jerusalem. *Isaiah 66:13, NIV*

For men are not cast off by the LORD forever. Though he brings grief, he will show compassion, so great is his unfailing love. For he does not willingly bring affliction or grief to the children of men. *Lamentations 3:31-33, NIV*

Now may our Lord Jesus Christ Himself, and our God and Father, who has loved us and given us everlasting consolation and good hope by grace, comfort your hearts and establish you in every good word and work. *2 Thessalonians 2:16-17, NKJ*

Burst into songs of joy together, you ruins of Jerusalem, for the LORD has comforted his people, he has redeemed Jerusalem. *Isaiah 52:9, NIV*

As a father has compassion on his children, so the LORD has compassion on those who fear him; for he knows how we are formed, he remembers that we are dust. *Psalm 103:13-14, NIV*

God Is Faithful

"*Extraordinary afflictions are not always the punishment of extraordinary sins, but sometimes the trial of extraordinary graces.—Sanctified afflictions are spiritual promotions.*"

MATTHEW HENRY

God is faithful, by whom you were called into the fellowship of His Son, Jesus Christ our Lord. *1 Corinthians 1:9, NKJ*

For the word of the LORD is right and true; he is faithful in all he does. *Psalm 33:4, NIV*

If we confess our sins, He is faithful and just to forgive us our sins and to cleanse us from all unrighteousness. *1 John 1:9, NKJ*

I know, O LORD, that Your judgments are right, and that in faithfulness You have afflicted me. Let, I pray, Your merciful kindness be for my comfort, according to Your word to Your servant. *Psalm 119:75-76, NKJ*

Surely goodness and mercy shall follow me all the days of my life; and I will dwell in the house of the LORD forever. *Psalm 23:6, NKJ*

Your faithfulness extends to every generation, like the earth you created; it endures by your decree, for everything serves your plans. *Psalm 119:90-91, TLB*

But the Lord is faithful, and he will strengthen and protect you from the evil one. *2 Thessalonians 3:3, NIV*

It is the living who give thanks to Thee, as I do today; a father tells his sons about Thy faithfulness. *Isaiah 38:19, NASB*

A bruised reed he will not break, and a smoldering wick he will not snuff out. *Isaiah 42:3, NIV*

Let us hold fast the confession of our hope without wavering, for He who promised is faithful . . . *Hebrews 10:23, NASB*

I will praise you with the harp for your faithfulness, O my God; I will sing praise to you with the lyre, O

Holy One of Israel. My lips will shout for joy when I sing praise to you—I, whom you have redeemed. *Psalm 71:22-23, NIV*

Through the LORD's mercies we are not consumed, because His compassions fail not. They are new every morning; great is Your faithfulness. "The LORD is my portion," says my soul, "Therefore I hope in Him!" *Lamentations 3:22-24, NKJ*

But you, O Lord, are a compassionate and gracious God, slow to anger, abounding in love and faithfulness. *Psalm 86:15, NIV*

Cast your burden upon the LORD, and He will sustain you; He will never allow the righteous to be shaken. *Psalm 55:22, NASB*

God Comforts Us through His People

"Rejoice with those who rejoice; mourn with those who mourn."

APOSTLE PAUL

But one who prophesies, preaching the messages of God, is helping others grow in the LORD, encouraging and comforting them. *1 Corinthians 14:3, TLB*

But if we are afflicted, it is for your comfort and salvation; or if we are comforted, it is for your comfort, which is effective in the patient enduring of the same sufferings which we also suffer; and our hope for you is firmly grounded, knowing that as you are sharers of our sufferings, so also you are sharers of our comfort. *2 Corinthians 1:6-7, NASB*

But God, who comforts the depressed, comforted us by the coming of Titus; and not only by his coming, but also by the comfort with which he was comforted in you, as he reported to us your longing, your mourning, your zeal for me; so that I rejoiced even more. *2 Corinthians 7:6-7, NASB*

Then I will give you shepherds after my own heart, who will lead you with knowledge and understanding. *Jeremiah 3:15*, NIV

For we have great joy and consolation in your love, because the hearts of the saints have been refreshed by you, brother. *Philemon 1:7*, NKJ

But encourage one another daily, as long as it is called Today, so that none of you may be hardened by sin's deceitfulness. *Hebrews 3:13*, NIV

Let us not give up meeting together, as some are in the habit of doing, but let us encourage one another—and all the more as you see the Day approaching. *Hebrews 10:25*, NIV

Because of my chains, most of the brothers in the Lord have been encouraged to speak the word of God more courageously and fearlessly. *Philippians 1:14*, NIV

This is what I have asked of God for you: that you will be encouraged and knit together by strong ties of love, and that you will have the rich experience of knowing Christ with real certainty and clear understanding. For God's secret plan, now at last made known, is Christ himself. *Colossians 2:2, TLB*

For I long to see you in order that I may impart some spiritual gift to you, that you may be established; that is, that I may be encouraged together with you while among you, each of us by the other's faith, both yours and mine. *Romans 1:11-12, NASB*

... who comforts us in all our affliction so that we may be able to comfort those who are in any affliction with the comfort with which we ourselves are comforted by God. *2 Corinthians 1:4, NASB*

We sent Timothy, who is our brother and God's fellow worker in spreading the gospel of Christ, to strengthen and encourage you in your faith ... *1 Thessalonians 3:2, NIV*

For just as the sufferings of Christ flow over into our lives, so also through Christ our comfort overflows. *2 Corinthians 1:5, NIV*

Therefore comfort each other and edify one another, just as you also are doing. *1 Thessalonians 5:11, NKJ*

Now we exhort you, brethren, warn those who are unruly, comfort the fainthearted, uphold the weak, be patient with all. *1 Thessalonians 5:14, NKJ*

But my mouth would encourage you; comfort from my lips would bring you relief. *Job 16:5, NIV*

. . . learn to do right! Seek justice, encourage the oppressed. Defend the cause of the fatherless, plead the case of the widow. *Isaiah 1:17, NIV*

God Comforts Us through His Word

"The Bible is the window in this prison world, through which we may look into eternity."

TIMOTHY DWIGHT

This is my comfort in my affliction, for your word has given me life. *Psalm 119:50, NKJ*

I remember your ancient laws, O LORD, and I find comfort in them. *Psalm 119:52, NIV*

For whatever things were written before were written for our learning, that we through the patience and comfort of the Scriptures might have hope. *Romans 15:4, NKJ*

Every word of God is pure; he is a shield to those who put their trust in Him. *Proverbs 30:5, NKJ*

My soul melts from heaviness; strengthen me according to Your word. *Psalm 119:28, NKJ*

May I never forget your words; for they are my only hope. *Psalm 119:43, TLB*

Never forget your promises to me your servant, for they are my only hope. They give me strength in all my troubles; how they refresh and revive me! *Psalm 119:49-50, TLB*

For these laws of yours have been my source of joy and singing through all these years of my earthly pilgrimage. *Psalm 119:54, TLB*

If your law had not been my delight, I would have perished in my affliction. *Psalm 119:92, NIV*

Those who love your laws have great peace of heart and mind and do not stumble. *Psalm 119:165, TLB*

The whole Bible was given to us by inspiration from God and is useful to teach us what is true and to make us realize what is wrong in our lives; it straightens us out and helps us do what is right. It is God's way of making us well prepared at every point, fully equipped to do good to everyone. *2 Timothy 3:16-17, TLB*

God Delivers
His People

"When through the deep waters
I call thee to go,
The rivers of sorrow shall not overflow;
For I will be with thee,
thy troubles to bless,
And sanctify to thee thy deepest distress.

"When through fiery trials
thy pathway shall lie,
My grace, all-sufficient,
shall be thy supply;
The flame shall not hurt thee;
I only design
Thy dross to consume,
and thy gold to refine."

AMERICAN HYMN:
"How Firm a Foundation"

But those who suffer he delivers in their suffering; he speaks to them in their affliction. *Job 36:15, NIV*

The Lord will rescue me from every evil attack and will bring me safely to his heavenly kingdom. To him be glory for ever and ever. Amen. *2 Timothy 4:18, NIV*

Return, O LORD, deliver me! Oh, save me for Your mercies' sake! *Psalm 6:4, NKJ*

Our fathers trusted in You; they trusted, and You delivered them. *Psalm 22:4, NKJ*

I sought the LORD, and he answered me; he delivered me from all my fears. *Psalm 34:4, NIV*

For the Angel of the Lord guards and rescues all who reverence him. *Psalm 34:7, TLB*

The righteous cry out, and the LORD hears them; he delivers them from all their troubles. *Psalm 34:17, NIV*

The good man does not escape all troubles—he has them too. But the LORD helps him in each and every one. *Psalm 34:19, TLB*

For great is your love toward me; you have delivered me from the depths of the grave. *Psalm 86:13, NIV*

He shall call upon Me, and I will answer him; I will be with him in trouble; I will deliver him and honor him. *Psalm 91:15, NKJ*

For you, O LORD, have delivered my soul from death, my eyes from tears, my feet from stumbling . . . *Psalm 116:8, NIV*

He has delivered us from such a deadly peril, and he will deliver us. On him we have set our hope that he will continue to deliver us . . . *2 Corinthians 1:10, NIV*

You have let me sink down deep in desperate problems. But you will bring me back to life again, up from the depths of the earth. You will give me greater honor than before, and turn again and comfort me. *Psalm 71:20-21, TLB*

"But I will deliver you in that day," says the LORD, "and you shall not be given into the hand of the men of whom you are afraid. For I will surely deliver you, and you shall not fall by the sword; but your life shall be as a prize to you, because you have put your trust in Me," says the LORD. *Jeremiah 39:17-18, NKJ*

But you, O Sovereign LORD, deal well with me for your name's sake; out of the goodness of your love, deliver me. *Psalm 109:21, NIV*

God Heals Our Diseases

"Although today He prunes
my twigs with pain,
Yet doth His blood nourish and
warm my root:
Tomorrow I shall put forth buds again
And clothe myself with fruit."

**CHRISTINA GEORGINA
ROSSETTI:**
From House to House

O LORD my God, I cried out to You, and you healed me. *Psalm 30:2, NKJ*

And great multitudes came to Him, bringing with them those who were lame, crippled, blind, dumb, and many others, and they laid them down at His feet; and He healed them . . . *Matthew 15:30, NASB*

See now that I myself am He! There is no god besides me. I put to death and I bring to life, I have wounded and I will heal, and no one can deliver out of my hand. *Deuteronomy 32:39, NIV*

You brought me back from the brink of the grave, from death itself, and here I am alive! *Psalm 30:3, TLB*

Praise the LORD, O my soul, and forget not all his benefits—who forgives all your sins and heals all your diseases . . . *Psalm 103:2-3, NIV*

He heals the brokenhearted and binds up their wounds. *Psalm 147:3, NIV*

But He was wounded for our transgressions, He was bruised for our iniquities; the chastisement for our peace was upon Him, and by His stripes we are healed. *Isaiah 53:5, NKJ*

Then your light shall break forth like the morning, your healing shall spring forth speedily, and your righteousness shall go before you; the glory of the LORD shall be your rear guard. *Isaiah 58:8, NKJ*

Heal me, O LORD, and I will be healed; save me and I will be saved, for you are the one I praise. *Jeremiah 17:14, NIV*

Come, let us return to the LORD. He has torn us to pieces but he will heal us; he has injured us but he will bind up our wounds. *Hosea 6:1, NIV*

But for you who fear my name, the Sun of Righteousness will rise with healing in his wings. And you will go free, leaping with joy like calves let out to pasture. *Malachi 4:2, TLB*

I said, "LORD, be merciful to me; heal my soul, for I have sinned against You." *Psalm 41:4, NKJ*

When Jesus landed and saw a large crowd, he had compassion on them and healed their sick. *Matthew 14:14, NIV*

"Daughter," he said to her, "your faith has healed you. Go in peace." *Luke 8:48, TLB*

Jesus called his twelve disciples to him, and gave them authority to cast out evil spirits and to heal every kind of sickness and disease. *Matthew 10:1, TLB*

Therefore confess your sins to each other and pray for each other so that you may be healed. The prayer of a righteous man is powerful and effective. *James 5:16, NIV*

And He Himself bore our sins in His body on the cross, that we might die to sin and live to righteousness; for by His wounds you were healed. *1 Peter 2:24, NASB*

God Gives Hope

*"My hope is built on nothing less
Than Jesus' blood and righteousness;
I dare not trust the sweetest frame,
But wholly lean on Jesus' name.*

*"When darkness veils His lovely face,
I rest on His unchanging grace;
In every high and stormy gale,
My anchor holds within the veil."*

EDWARD MOTE:
"My Hope is Built on Nothing Less"

No one whose hope is in you will ever be put to shame, but they will be put to shame who are treacherous without excuse. *Psalm 25:3,* NIV

. . . guide me in your truth and teach me, for you are God my Savior, and my hope is in you all day long. *Psalm 25:5,* NIV

Be joyful in hope, patient in affliction, faithful in prayer. *Romans 12:12,* NIV

Behold, the eye of the LORD is on those who fear Him, on those who hope in His mercy . . . *Psalm 33:18,* NKJ

Why are you cast down, O my soul? And why are you disquieted within me? Hope in God; for I shall yet praise Him, the help of my countenance and my God. *Psalm 42:11,* NKJ

I will praise you forever for what you have done; in your name I will hope, for your name is good. I will praise

you in the presence of your saints.
Psalm 52:9, NIV

There is surely a future hope for you,
and your hope will not be cut off.
Proverbs 23:18, NIV

. . . but those who hope in the LORD
will renew their strength. They will
soar on wings like eagles; they will
run and not grow weary, they will
walk and not be faint. *Isaiah 40:31, NIV*

For I know the thoughts that I think
toward you, says the LORD, thoughts
of peace and not of evil, to give you a
future and a hope. *Jeremiah 29:11, NKJ*

. . . and hope does not disappoint;
because the love of God has been
poured out within our hearts through
the Holy Spirit who was given to us.
Romans 5:5, NASB

We wait in hope for the LORD; he is our
help and our shield. *Psalm 33:20, NIV*

This certain hope of being saved is a strong and trustworthy anchor for our souls, connecting us with God himself . . . *Hebrews 6:19a, TLB*

Blessed be the God and Father of our Lord Jesus Christ, who according to His great mercy has caused us to be born again to a living hope through the resurrection of Jesus Christ from the dead, to obtain an inheritance which is imperishable and undefiled and will not fade away, reserved in heaven for you . . . *1 Peter 1:3-4, NASB*

May the God of hope fill you with all joy and peace as you trust in him, so that you may overflow with hope by the power of the Holy Spirit. *Romans 15:13, NIV*

God Gives Joy

"Joy is the echo of God's life within us."

JOSEPH MARMION:
Orthodoxy

*"Joy to the world! the Lord is come; Let
earth receive her King."*

ISAAC WATTS:
Psalm XCVIII, st 1

For you shall go out with joy, and be led out with peace; the mountains and the hills shall break forth into singing before you, and all the trees of the field shall clap their hands. *Isaiah 55:12, NKJ*

But let all those rejoice who put their trust in You; let them ever shout for joy, because You defend them; let those also who love Your name be joyful in You. *Psalm 5:11, NKJ*

You have made known to me the path of life; you will fill me with joy in your presence, with eternal pleasures at your right hand. *Psalm 16:11, NIV*

For His anger is but for a moment, His favor is for life; weeping may endure for a night, but joy comes in the morning. *Psalm 30:5, NKJ*

But the fruit of the Spirit is love, joy, peace, patience, kindness, goodness, faithfulness, gentleness and self-control. Against such things there is no law. *Galatians 5:22-23, NIV*

Those who sow in tears shall reap in joy. *Psalm 126:5, NKJ*

So the ransomed of the LORD shall return, and come to Zion with singing, with everlasting joy on their heads. They shall obtain joy and gladness; sorrow and sighing shall flee away. *Isaiah 51:11, NKJ*

Therefore with joy you will draw water from the wells of salvation. *Isaiah 12:3, NKJ*

These things I have spoken to you, that My joy may be in you, and that your joy may be made full. *John 15:11, NASB*

Until now you have not asked for anything in my name. Ask and you will receive, and your joy will be complete. *John 16:24, NIV*

You have made known to me the ways of life; you will make me full of joy in your presence. *Acts 2:28, NKJ*

God Delights to Show Mercy

"There's a wideness in God's mercy
Like the wideness of the sea;
There's a kindness in His justice
Which is more than liberty."

FREDERICK WILLIAM FABER

Mercy, peace, and love be multiplied to you. *Jude 1:2, NKJ*

I love the LORD, for he heard my voice; he heard my cry for mercy. *Psalm 116:1, NIV*

But God, being rich in mercy, because of His great love with which He loved us, even when we were dead in our transgressions, made us alive together with Christ (by grace you have been saved) . . . *Ephesians 2:4-5, NASB*

Let, I pray, Your merciful kindness be for my comfort, according to Your word to Your servant. *Psalm 119:76, NKJ*

Blessed be the God and Father of our Lord Jesus Christ, who according to His abundant mercy has begotten us again to a living hope through the resurrection of Jesus Christ from the dead . . . *1 Peter 1:3, NKJ*

The LORD takes pleasure in those who fear Him, in those who hope in His mercy. *Psalm 147:11*, NKJ

Let the wicked forsake his way, and the unrighteous man his thoughts; let him return to the LORD, and He will have mercy on him; and to our God, for He will abundantly pardon. *Isaiah 55:7*, NKJ

In all their distress he too was distressed, and the angel of his presence saved them. In his love and mercy he redeemed them; he lifted them up and carried them all the days of old. *Isaiah 63:9*, NIV

Who is a God like you, who pardons sin and forgives the transgression of the remnant of his inheritance? You do not stay angry forever but delight to show mercy. *Micah 7:18*, NIV

The LORD has heard my cry for mercy; the LORD accepts my prayer. *Psalm 6:9*, NIV

Blessed are the merciful, for they shall receive mercy. *Matthew 5:7*, NASB

And His mercy is upon generation after generation towards those who fear Him. *Luke 1:50*, NASB

. . . not by works of righteousness which we have done, but according to His mercy He saved us, through the washing of regeneration and renewing of the Holy Spirit . . . *Titus 3:5*, NKJ

Let us therefore come boldly to the throne of grace, that we may obtain mercy and find grace to help in time of need. *Hebrews 4:16*, NKJ

Once you were not a people, but now you are the people of God; once you had not received mercy, but now you have received mercy. *1 Peter 2:10*, NIV

Keep yourselves in God's love as you wait for the mercy of our Lord Jesus Christ to bring you to eternal life. *Jude 1:21*, NIV

God Comforts Those Who Mourn

*"Earth has no sorrow
that Heaven cannot heal."*

SIR THOMAS MOORE:
Come, Ye Disconsolate

"Comfort, yes, comfort My people!" says your God. *Isaiah 40:1, NKJ*

Truly, truly, I say to you, that you will weep and lament, but the world will rejoice; you will be sorrowful, but your sorrow will be turned to joy. *John 16:20, NASB*

Blessed are those who mourn, for they will be comforted. *Matthew 5:4, NIV*

For the Lamb in the center of the throne shall be their shepherd, and shall guide them to springs of the water of life; and God shall wipe every tear from their eyes. *Revelation 7:17, NASB*

And the ransomed of the LORD shall return, and come to Zion with singing, with everlasting joy on their heads. They shall obtain joy and gladness, and sorrow and sighing shall flee away. *Isaiah 35:10, NKJ*

Then maidens will dance and be glad, young men and old as well. I will turn their mourning into gladness; I will give them comfort and joy instead of sorrow. *Jeremiah 31:13*, NIV

I will rejoice in Jerusalem, and joy in My people; the voice of weeping shall no longer be heard in her, nor the voice of crying. *Isaiah 65:19*, NKJ

The Spirit of the Sovereign LORD is on me, because the LORD has anointed me to preach good news to the poor. He has sent me to bind up the broken-hearted, to proclaim freedom for the captives and release from darkness for the prisoners, to proclaim the year of the LORD's favor and the day of vengeance of our God, to comfort all who mourn, and provide for those who grieve in Zion—to bestow on them a crown of beauty instead of ashes, the oil of gladness instead of mourning, and a garment of praise instead of a spirit of despair. *Isaiah 61:1-3a*, NIV

O my Comforter in sorrow, my heart is faint within me. *Jeremiah 8:18, NIV*

And when the Lord saw her, He felt compassion for her, and said to her, "Do not weep." *Luke 7:13, NASB*

Let not your heart be troubled. You are trusting God, now trust in me. *John 14:1, TLB*

The LORD will protect you from all evil; He will keep your soul. The LORD will guard your going out and your coming in from this time forth and forever. *Psalm 121:7-8, NASB*

God Gives Patience in Suffering

"God says, 'To me your trouble is only a point, a moment, a drop, a spark.' But reason converts a mathematical point into an infinite line, because it does not see the end of the affliction."

MARTIN LUTHER

The LORD is good to those who wait
for Him, to the soul who seeks Him. It
is good that one should hope and wait
quietly for the salvation of the LORD.
Lamentations 3:25-26, NKJ

But the fruit of the Spirit is love, joy,
peace, patience, kindness, goodness,
faithfulness . . . *Galatians 5:22, NASB*

For examples of patience in suffering,
look at the Lord's prophets. We know
how happy they are now because they
stayed true to him then, even though
they suffered greatly for it. Job is an
example of a man who continued to
trust the Lord in sorrow; from his ex-
periences we can see how the Lord's
plan finally ended in good, for he is
full of tenderness and mercy. *James
5:10-11, TLB*

Let this encourage God's people to
endure patiently every trial and per-
secution, for they are his saints who
remain firm to the end in obedience to

his commands and trust in Jesus. *Revelation 14:12, TLB*

Since you have kept my command to endure patiently, I will also keep you from the hour of trial that is going to come upon the whole world to test those who live on the earth. *Revelation 3:10, NIV*

Be joyful in hope, patient in affliction, faithful in prayer. *Romans 12:12, NIV*

Perseverance must finish its work so that you may be mature and complete, not lacking anything. *James 1:4, NIV*

I waited patiently for the LORD; he turned to me and heard my cry. *Psalm 40:1, NIV*

May the God who gives endurance and encouragement give you a spirit of unity among yourselves as you follow Christ Jesus . . . *Romans 15:5, NIV*

God Comforts
the Poor

*"For whatever reason God chose to make
man as he is—limited and suffering and
subject to sorrows and death—He had the
honesty and courage to take His own
medicine. . . . He has Himself gone
through the whole of human experience,
from the trivial irritations of family life
and the cramping restrictions of hard
work and lack of money to the worst
horrors of pain and humiliation, defeat,
despair, and death. When He was a man,
He played the man. He was born in
poverty and died in disgrace and thought
it well worthwhile."*

DOROTHY L. SAYERS:
*Christian Letters to a Post-Christian
World*

The lowly he sets on high, and those who mourn are lifted to safety. *Job 5:11*, NIV

For the needy shall not always be forgotten; the expectation of the poor shall not perish forever. *Psalm 9:18*, NKJ

He is the refuge of the poor and humble when evildoers are oppressing them. *Psalm 14:6*, TLB

This poor man cried to the Lord—and the Lord heard him and saved him out of his troubles. *Psalm 34:6*, TLB

My whole being will exclaim, "Who is like you, O LORD? You rescue the poor from those too strong for them, the poor and needy from those who rob them." *Psalm 35:10*, NIV

I am poor and needy, yet the Lord is thinking about me right now! O my God, you are my helper. You are my

Savior; come quickly, and save me. Please don't delay! *Psalm 40:17, TLB*

The poor will see and be glad—you who seek God, may your hearts live! *Psalm 69:32, NIV*

For He will deliver the needy when he cries, the poor also, and him who has no helper. *Psalm 72:12, NKJ*

I know that the LORD will maintain the cause of the afflicted, and justice for the poor. *Psalm 140:12, NKJ*

And turning His gaze on His disciples, He began to say, "Blessed are you who are poor, for yours is the kingdom of God." *Luke 6:20, NASB*

. . . but with righteousness he will judge the needy, with justice he will give decisions for the poor of the earth. He will strike the earth with the rod of his mouth; with the breath of his lips he will slay the wicked. *Isaiah 11:4, NIV*

The poorest of the poor will find pasture, and the needy will lie down in safety. *Isaiah 14:30a, NIV*

Listen, my dear brothers: Has not God chosen those who are poor in the eyes of the world to be rich in faith and to inherit the kingdom he promised those who love him? *James 2:5, NIV*

For You have been a strength to the poor, a strength to the needy in his distress, a refuge from the storm, a shade from the heat; for the blast of the terrible ones is as a storm against the wall. *Isaiah 25:4, NKJ*

The Spirit of the Lord GOD is upon Me, because the LORD has anointed Me to preach good tidings to the poor; He has sent Me to heal the brokenhearted, to proclaim liberty to the captives, and the opening of the prison to those who are bound . . . *Isaiah 61:1, NKJ*

"He defended the cause of the poor and needy, and so all went well. Is that not what it means to know me?" declares the LORD. *Jeremiah 22:16, NIV*

Once more the humble will rejoice in the LORD; the needy will rejoice in the Holy One of Israel. *Isaiah 29:19, NIV*

For you know the grace of our Lord Jesus Christ, that though he was rich, yet for your sakes he became poor, so that you through his poverty might become rich. *2 Corinthians 8:9, NIV*

As it is written: "He has scattered abroad his gifts to the poor; his righteousness endures forever." *2 Corinthians 9:9, NIV*

The poor shall eat and be satisfied; all who seek the LORD shall find him and shall praise his name. Their hearts shall rejoice with everlasting joy. *Psalm 22:26, TLB*

God Desires Praise in Affliction

*"What language shall I borrow
to thank Thee, dearest Friend,
For this Thy dying sorrow,
Thy pity without end?
O make me Thine forever;
And should I fainting be,
Lord, let me never, never
Outlive my love for Thee."*

ANONYMOUS:
"O Sacred Head Now Wounded"

My heart is steadfast, O God, my heart is steadfast; I will sing and give praise. *Psalm 57:7, NKJ*

"Naked I came from my mother's womb, and naked I will depart. The LORD gave and the LORD has taken away; may the name of the LORD be praised." *Job 1:21, NIV*

Why are you in despair, O my soul? And why have you become disturbed within me? Hope in God, for I shall again praise Him for the help of His presence. *Psalm 42:5, NASB*

On that day you will say, "Praise the Lord! He was angry with me, but now he comforts me." *Isaiah 12:1, TLB*

Sing, O heavens! Be joyful, O earth! And break out in singing, O mountains! For the LORD has comforted His people, and will have mercy on His afflicted. *Isaiah 49:13, NKJ*

But at midnight Paul and Silas were praying and singing hymns to God, and the prisoners were listening to them. *Acts 16:25, NKJ*

Praise be to the God and Father of our Lord Jesus Christ, who has blessed us in the heavenly realms with every spiritual blessing in Christ. *Ephesians 1:3, NIV*

But I have trusted in Your mercy; my heart shall rejoice in Your salvation. I will sing to the LORD, because He has dealt bountifully with me. *Psalm 13:5-6, NKJ*

Therefore by Him let us continually offer the sacrifice of praise to God, that is, the fruit of our lips, giving thanks to His name. *Hebrews 13:15, NKJ*

Is anyone among you suffering? He should keep on praying about it. And those who have reason to be thankful should continually be singing praises to the Lord. *James 5:13, TLB*

Rejoice in the Lord always; again I will say, rejoice! *Philippians 4:4, NASB*

However, if you suffer as a Christian, do not be ashamed, but praise God that you bear that name. *1 Peter 4:16, NIV*

Record my lament; list my tears on your scroll—are they not in your record? Then my enemies will turn back when I call for help. By this I will know that God is for me. In God, whose word I praise, in the LORD, whose word I praise—in God I trust; I will not be afraid. What can man do to me? *Psalm 56:8-11, NIV*

These have come so that your faith—of greater worth than gold, which perishes even though refined by fire—may be proved genuine and may result in praise, glory and honor when Jesus Christ is revealed. *1 Peter 1:7, NIV*

God Hears
Prayer in
Affliction

---

*"The best prayers have often more groans
than words."*

JOHN BUNYAN

*"In suffering one learns to pray
best of all."*

HAROLD A. BOSLEY:
On Final Ground

As for me, I will call upon God, and the LORD shall save me. Evening and morning and at noon I will pray, and cry aloud, and He shall hear my voice. *Psalm 55:16-17, NKJ*

Bless those who curse you, pray for those who mistreat you. *Luke 6:28, NASB*

Pray all the time. Ask God for anything in line with the Holy Spirit's wishes. Plead with him, reminding him of your needs, and keep praying earnestly for all Christians everywhere. *Ephesians 6:18, TLB*

I pray for them. I do not pray for the world but for those whom You have given Me, for they are Yours. *John 17:9, NKJ*

Peter was therefore kept in prison, but constant prayer was offered to God for him by the church. *Acts 12:5, NKJ*

Likewise the Spirit also helps in our weaknesses. For we do not know what we should pray for as we ought, but the Spirit Himself makes intercession for us with groanings which cannot be uttered. *Romans 8:26, NKJ*

Therefore, confess your sins to one another, and pray for one another, so that you may be healed. The effective prayer of a righteous man can accomplish much. *James 5:16, NASB*

Be joyful in hope, patient in affliction, faithful in prayer. *Romans 12:12, NIV*

Don't worry about anything; instead, pray about everything; tell God your needs and don't forget to thank him for his answers. *Philippians 4:6, TLB*

Devote yourselves to prayer, being watchful and thankful. *Colossians 4:2, NIV*

I pray that out of his glorious riches he may strengthen you with power through his Spirit in your inner being . . . *Ephesians 3:16, NIV*

During the days of Jesus' life on earth, he offered up prayers and petitions with loud cries and tears to the one who could save him from death, and he was heard because of his reverent submission. *Hebrews 5:7*, NIV

Is any one of you in trouble? He should pray. Is anyone happy? Let him sing songs of praise. Is any one of you sick? He should call the elders of the church to pray over him and anoint him with oil in the name of the Lord. *James 5:13*, NIV

The smoke of the incense, together with the prayers of the saints, went up before God from the angel's hand. *Revelation 8:4*, NIV

Call upon Me in the day of trouble; I will deliver you, and you shall glorify Me. *Psalm 50:15*, NKJ

For the Lord is watching his children, listening to their prayers . . . *1 Peter 3:12a*, TLB

God Provides
for Our Needs

*"How calmly may we commit ourselves
to the hands of Him who bears up
the world."*

JEAN PAUL RICHTER

The eyes of all look expectantly to You, and You give them their food in due season. You open Your hand and satisfy the desire of every living thing. *Psalm 145:15-16, NKJ*

You gave me life and showed me kindness, and in your providence watched over my spirit. *Job 10:12, NIV*

He gives food to those who trust him; he never forgets his promises. *Psalm 111:5, TLB*

He provided redemption for his people; he ordained his covenant forever—holy and awesome is his name. *Psalm 111:9, NIV*

Yet he has not left himself without testimony: He has shown kindness by giving you rain from heaven and crops in their seasons; he provides you with plenty of food and fills your hearts with joy. *Acts 14:17, NIV*

The LORD will open the heavens, the storehouse of his bounty, to send rain on your land in season and to bless all the work of your hands. You will lend to many nations but will borrow from none. *Deuteronomy 28:12, NIV*

You care for the land and water it; you enrich it abundantly. The streams of God are filled with water to provide the people with grain, for so you have ordained it. *Psalm 65:9, NIV*

Forty years You sustained them in the wilderness; they lacked nothing; their clothes did not wear out and their feet did not swell. *Nehemiah 9:21, NKJ*

So don't worry at all about having enough food and clothing. Why be like the heathen? For they take pride in all these things and are deeply concerned about them. But your heavenly Father already knows perfectly well that you need them, and he will give them to you if you give him first place in your life and live as he wants you to. *Matthew 6:31-33, TLB*

His divine power has given us everything we need for life and godliness through our knowledge of him who called us by his own glory and goodness. Through these he has given us his very great and precious promises, so that through them you may participate in the divine nature and escape the corruption in the world caused by evil desires. *2 Peter 1:3-4, NIV*

And my God shall supply all your needs according to His riches in glory in Christ Jesus. *Philippians 4:19, NASB*

God is able to make it up to you by giving you everything you need and more, so that there will not only be enough for your own needs, but plenty left over to give joyfully to others. *2 Corinthians 9:8, TLB*

God Adds Purpose to Our Suffering

*"Troubles are often the tools by which
God fashions us for better things."*

HENRY WARD BEECHER

There is an appointed time for everything. And there is a time for every event under heaven. *Ecclesiastes 3:1, NASB*

Before I was afflicted I went astray, but now I keep Thy word. *Psalm 119:67, NASB*

We can rejoice, too, when we run into problems and trials for we know that they are good for us—they help us learn to be patient. And patience develops strength of character in us and helps us trust God more each time we use it until finally our hope and faith are strong and steady. *Romans 5:3-4, TLB*

And you shall remember that the LORD your God led you all the way these forty years in the wilderness, to humble you and test you, to know what was in your heart, whether you would keep His commandments or not . . . For the LORD your God is

bringing you into a good land . . .
Deuteronomy 8:2, 7a, NKJ

He is the LORD; let him do what is good in his eyes. *1 Samuel 3:18b, NIV*

Surely it was for my benefit that I suffered such anguish. In your love you kept me from the pit of destruction; you have put all my sins behind your back. *Isaiah 38:17, NIV*

Being punished isn't enjoyable while it is happening—it hurts! But afterwards we can see the result, a quiet growth in grace and character. *Hebrews 12:11, TLB*

Behold, I will do a new thing, now it shall spring forth; shall you not know it? I will even make a road in the wilderness and rivers in the desert. *Isaiah 43:19, NKJ*

"For my thoughts are not your thoughts, nor are your ways My ways," says the LORD. "For as the heavens are higher than the earth, so are My ways higher than your ways, and My thoughts than your thoughts." *Isaiah 55:8-9, NKJ*

Behold, happy is the man whom God corrects; therefore do not despise the chastening of the Almighty. For He bruises, but He binds up; He wounds, but His hands make whole. *Job 5:17-18, NKJ*

And He said to me, "My grace is sufficient for you, for My strength is made perfect in weakness." Therefore most gladly I will rather boast in my infirmities, that the power of Christ may rest upon me. Therefore I take pleasure in infirmities, in reproaches, in needs, in persecutions, in distresses, for Christ's sake. For when I am weak, then I am strong. *2 Corinthians 12:9-10, NKJ*

Endure hardship as discipline; God is treating you as sons. For what son is not disciplined by his father? *Hebrews 12:7, NIV*

Consider it pure joy, my brothers, whenever you face trials of many kinds, because you know that the testing of your faith develops perseverance. *James 1:2-3, NIV*

But rejoice that you participate in the sufferings of Christ, so that you may be overjoyed when his glory is revealed. *1 Peter 4:13, NIV*

Now if we are children, then we are heirs—heirs of God and co-heirs with Christ, if indeed we share in his sufferings in order that we may also share in his glory. I consider that our present sufferings are not worth comparing with the glory that will be revealed in us. *Romans 8:17-18, NIV*

Indeed, in our hearts we felt the sentence of death. But this happened that we might not rely on ourselves but on God, who raises the dead. *2 Corinthians 1:9, NIV*

God Is Our Refuge

"When outward strength is broken, faith rests on the promises. In the midst of sorrow, faith draws the sting out of every trouble, and takes out the bitterness from every affliction."

ROBERT CECIL

For in the day of trouble he will keep me safe in his dwelling; he will hide me in the shelter of his tabernacle and set me high upon a rock. *Psalm 27:5, NIV*

The eternal God is your refuge, and underneath are the everlasting arms; He will thrust out the enemy from before you, and will say "Destroy!" *Deuteronomy 33:27, NKJ*

The LORD also will be a refuge for the oppressed, a refuge in times of trouble. *Psalm 9:9, NKJ*

The LORD is my rock and my fortress and my deliverer; my God, my strength, in whom I will trust; my shield and the horn of my salvation, my stronghold. *Psalm 18:2, NKJ*

You are my hiding place; you will protect me from trouble and surround me with songs of deliverance. *Psalm 32:7, NIV*

God is our refuge and strength, a very present help in trouble. *Psalm 46:1, NKJ*

The LORD of hosts is with us; the God of Jacob is our refuge. *Psalm 46:7, NKJ*

Be gracious to me, O God, be gracious to me, for my soul takes refuge in Thee; and in the shadow of Thy wings I will take refuge, until destruction passes by. *Psalm 57:1, NASB*

But I will sing of your strength, in the morning I will sing of your love; for you are my fortress, my refuge in times of trouble. *Psalm 59:16, NIV*

Yes, he alone is my Rock, my rescuer, defense and fortress—why then should I be tense with fear when troubles come? *Psalm 62:6, TLB*

My salvation and my honor depend on God; he is my mighty rock, my refuge. Trust in him at all times, O people; pour out your hearts to him, for God is our refuge. *Psalm 62:7-8, NIV*

. . . that by two immutable things, in which it is impossible for God to lie, we might have strong consolation, who have fled for refuge to lay hold of the hope set before us. *Hebrews 6:18, NKJ*

He is my loving God and my fortress, my stronghold and my deliverer, my shield, in whom I take refuge, who subdues peoples under me. *Psalm 144:2, NIV*

He who fears the LORD has a secure fortress, and for his children it will be a refuge. *Proverbs 14:26, NIV*

O LORD, my strength and my stronghold, and my refuge in the day of distress . . . *Jeremiah 16:19a, NASB*

The LORD is good, a refuge in times of trouble. He cares for those who trust in him . . . *Nahum 1:7, NIV*

God Comforts the Repentant Sinner

"*Our heavenly Father loves us too much to permit us to be rebels, so he chastens us that we might conform to his will . . . God's purpose is not to persecute us, but to perfect us. Chastening is not the work of an angry judge as he punishes a criminal. It is the work of a loving Father as he perfects a child.*"

WARREN W. WIERSBE:
Strategy of Satan

. . . if my people, who are called by my name, will humble themselves and pray and seek my face and turn from their wicked ways, then will I hear from heaven and will forgive their sin and will heal their land. *2 Chronicles 7:14, NIV*

For thus says the high and exalted One who lives forever, whose name is Holy, "I dwell on a high and holy place, and also with the contrite and lowly of spirit in order to revive the spirit of the lowly and to revive the heart of the contrite. *Isaiah 57:15, NASB*

They will come with weeping; they will pray as I bring them back. I will lead them beside streams of water on a level path where they will not stumble, because I am Israel's father, and Ephraim is my firstborn son. *Jeremiah 31:9, NIV*

I will heal their backsliding, I will love them freely, for My anger has turned away from him. *Hosea 14:4, NKJ*

And in that day you will say: "O
LORD, I will praise You; though You
were angry with me, Your anger is
turned away, and You comfort me.
Isaiah 12:1, NKJ

"For I have no pleasure in the death of
one who dies," says the Lord GOD.
"Therefore turn and live!" *Ezekiel
18:32, NKJ*

I tell you that in the same way there
will be more rejoicing in heaven over
one sinner who repents than over
ninety-nine righteous persons who do
not need to repent. *Luke 15:7, NIV*

Repent, then, and turn to God, so that
your sins may be wiped out, that
times of refreshing may come from
the Lord . . . *Acts 3:19, NIV*

Or do you think lightly of the riches of
His kindness and forbearance and
patience, not knowing that the kindness of God leads you to repentance?
Romans 2:4, NASB

For God sometimes uses sorrow in our lives to help us turn away from sin and seek eternal life. We should never regret his sending it. *2 Corinthians 7:10a, TLB*

Humble yourselves in the sight of the Lord, and He will lift you up. *James 4:10, NKJ*

The Lord is not slow in keeping his promise, as some understand slowness. He is patient with you, not wanting anyone to perish, but everyone to come to repentance. *2 Peter 3:9, NIV*

Those whom I love I rebuke and discipline. So be earnest, and repent. *Revelation 3:19, NIV*

He restores my soul; He leads me in the paths of righteousness for His name's sake. *Psalm 23:3, NKJ*

Though you have made me see troubles, many and bitter, you will restore my life again; from the depths of the earth you will again bring me up. *Psalm 71:20, NIV*

This is what the LORD says: "In the time of my favor I will answer you, and in the day of salvation I will help you; I will keep you and will make you to be a covenant for the people, to restore the land and to reassign its desolate inheritances . . . *Isaiah 49:8, NIV*

I have seen his ways, but I will heal him; I will guide him and restore comfort to him . . . *Isaiah 57:18, NIV*

Turn us back to You, O LORD, and we will be restored; renew our days as of old . . . *Lamentations 5:21, NKJ*

And the God of all grace, who called you to his eternal glory in Christ, after you have suffered a little while, will himself restore you and make you strong, firm and steadfast. *1 Peter 5:10, NIV*

God Gives Rest

"In his will is our peace."

ALIGHIERI DANTE:
Paradiso, Bk. III, I. 85

*"Thou hast touched me and I have been
translated into they peace."*

ST. AUGUSTINE:
Confessions, Bk. X, ch. 27

And He said, "My Presence will go with you, and I will give you rest." *Exodus 33:14*, NKJ

Blessed be the LORD, who has given rest to His people Israel, according to all that He promised. There has not failed one word of all His good promise, which He promised through His servant Moses. *1 Kings 8:56*, NKJ

Therefore my heart is glad and my tongue rejoices; my body also will rest secure . . . *Psalm 16:9* NIV

Find rest, O my soul, in God alone; my hope comes from him. *Psalm 62:5*, NIV

Now we who have believed enter that rest . . . *Hebrews 4:3a*, NIV

Be at rest once more, O my soul, for the LORD has been good to you. *Psalm 116:7*, NIV

This is what the Sovereign LORD, the Holy One of Israel, says:

"In repentance and rest is your salvation, in quietness and trust is your strength, but you would have none of it." *Isaiah 30:15, NIV*

Now may our Lord Jesus Christ Himself, and our God and Father, who has loved us and given us everlasting consolation and good hope by grace, comfort your hearts and establish you in every good word and work. *2 Thessalonians 2:16-17, NKJ*

Thus says the LORD: "Stand in the ways and see, and ask for the old paths, where the good way is, and walk in it; Then you will find rest for your souls. *Jeremiah 6:16a, NKJ*

Come to Me, all who are weary and heavy laden, and I will give you rest. Take My yoke upon you, and learn from Me, for I am gentle and humble in heart; and you shall find rest for your souls. For My yoke is easy, and My load is light. *Matthew 11:28-30, NASB*

But now the LORD my God has given me rest on every side, and there is no adversary or disaster. *1 Kings 5:4, NIV*

There remains therefore a rest for the people of God. *Hebrews 4:9, NKJ*

"I will feed My flock and I will lead them to rest," declares the Lord GOD. I will seek the lost, bring back the scattered, bind up the broken, and strengthen the sick . . . *Ezekiel 34:15-16a, NASB*

Do not be anxious about anything, but in everything, by prayer and petition, with thanksgiving, present your requests to God. And the peace of God, which transcends all understanding, will guard your hearts and your minds in Christ Jesus. *Philippians 4:6-7, NIV*

Now may the Lord of peace himself give you peace at all times and in every way. The Lord be with all of you. *2 Thessalonians 3:16, NIV*

God Enables Us to Overcome Temptation

"O to grace how great a debtor
Daily I'm constrained to be!
Let Thy goodness, like a fetter,
Bind my wandering heart to Thee:
Prone to wander, Lord, I feel it,
Prone to leave the God I love;
Here's my heart, O take and seal it,
Seal it for Thy courts above."

ROBERT ROBINSON:
"Come Thou Fount of Every Blessing"

For since He Himself was tempted in that which He has suffered, He is able to come to the aid of those who are tempted. *Hebrews 2:18, NASB*

No temptation has overtaken you but such as is common to man; and God is faithful, who will not allow you to be tempted beyond what you are able; but with the temptation will provide the way of escape also, that you may be able to endure it. *1 Corinthians 10:13, NASB*

For we do not have a High Priest who cannot sympathize with our weaknesses, but was in all points tempted as we are, yet without sin. Let us therefore come boldly to the throne of grace, that we may obtain mercy and find grace to help in time of need. *Hebrews 4:15-16, NKJ*

To him who is able to keep you from falling and to present you before his glorious presence without fault and with great joy—to the only God our

Savior be glory, majesty, power and authority, through Jesus Christ our Lord, before all ages, now and forevermore! Amen. *Jude 1:24, NIV*

And do not lead us into temptation, but deliver us from the evil one. *Matthew 6:13a, NKJ*

Keep watching and praying, that you may not come into temptation; the spirit is willing, but the flesh is weak. *Mark 14:38, NASB*

But I have prayed for you, that your faith should not fail; and when you have returned to Me, strengthen your brethren. *Luke 22:32, NKJ*

My prayer is not that you take them out of the world but that you protect them from the evil one. *John 17:15, NIV*

But the end of all things is at hand; therefore be serious and watchful in your prayers. *1 Peter 4:7, NKJ*

God Is with Us

"As sure as God puts his children into the
furnace of affliction,
he will be with them in it."

CHARLES HADDON SPURGEON

The LORD will guide you always; he will satisfy your needs in a sun-scorched land and will strengthen your frame. You will be like a well-watered garden, like a spring whose waters never fail. *Isaiah 58:11, NIV*

. . . and be sure of this—that I am with you always, even to the end of the world. *Matthew 28:20b, TLB*

In your unfailing love you will lead the people you have redeemed. In your strength you will guide them to your holy dwelling. *Exodus 15:13, NIV*

Yea, though I walk through the valley of the shadow of death, I will fear no evil; for You are with me; Your rod and Your staff, they comfort me. *Psalm 23:4, NKJ*

And I will ask the Father, and He will give you another Helper, that He may be with you forever; that is the Spirit of truth, whom the world cannot receive, because it does not behold

Him or know Him, but you know Him because He abides with you, and will be in you. *John 14:16-17, NASB*

Where can I go from Your Spirit? Or where can I flee from Your presence? If I ascend into heaven, You are there; if I make my bed in hell, behold, You are there. If I take the wings of the morning and dwell in the uttermost parts of the sea, even there Your hand shall lead me, and Your right hand shall hold me. *Psalm 139:7-10, NKJ*

Though he gave you the bread of adversity and water of affliction, yet he will be with you to teach you—with your own eyes you will see your Teacher. *Isaiah 30:20, TLB*

I will lead the blind by ways they have not known, along unfamiliar paths I will guide them; I will turn the darkness into light before them and make the rough places smooth. These are the things I will do; I will not forsake them. *Isaiah 42:16, NIV*

When you pass through the waters, I will be with you; and when you pass through the rivers, they will not sweep over you. When you walk through the fire, you will not be burned; the flames will not set you ablaze. *Isaiah 43:2, NIV*

The LORD Almighty is with us; the God of Jacob is our fortress. *Psalm 46:7, NIV*

In all their distress he too was distressed, and the angel of his presence saved them. In his love and mercy he redeemed them; he lifted them up and carried them all the days of old. *Isaiah 63:9, NIV*

The LORD your God is with you, he is mighty to save. He will take great delight in you, he will quiet you with his love, he will rejoice over you with singing. *Zephaniah 3:17, NIV*

I will not leave you as orphans; I will come to you. *John 14:18, NASB*

Prayers of Encouragement

"Prayer crowns God with the honor and glory due to His name, and God crowns prayer with assurance and comfort. The most praying souls are the most assured souls."

THOMAS BENTON BROOKS

While troubled or bereaved

Merciful Father, you have said in your Word that you do not willingly afflict or grieve us. Please remember me, Lord, in my sorrow. Help me bear this grief patiently. Comfort me with the sense of your goodness, and give me peace.

When in need of guidance

O God, you guide those who trust in you. Give me, in the midst of doubts and uncertain circumstances, the grace to seek your will. Save me from wrong choices. Help me to walk in your light and not to stumble.

In times of conflict

O God, you have bound us together in Christ. Help us in our struggles for justice and truth to confront one another without hatred or bitterness, and to work together. Give us the spiritual power to treat one another with forgiveness and respect. Please heal the wounds and break down the barriers that keep us from unity in Christ.

When needing peace

Dear God of peace, you have said that our strength will come from quietness of spirit and confidence in your power. By your Holy Spirit please hold me in your presence. Help me to be still and know you.

For the oppressed

Heavenly Father, it seems that I have no voice in this world and no power. I feel like a victim. There are those who have hurt me, cheated me, or taken advantage of me. May your Spirit give me strength and the power to forgive. Instill in me a sense of worth, and give me wisdom to speak with those who oppress me.

When in pain

Lord Jesus, by your patient suffering you gave dignity to earthly pain, and you gave us the example of obedience to your Father's will. Sustain me, by your grace, in my time of weakness and pain, that my strength and courage may not fail. Heal me according to your will, and help me to remember that this trial is small in comparison with my eternal life and glory in you.

When experiencing poverty

Lord Jesus, you have known poverty, and you care for those who are poor. Sustain me through this time of need. Teach me to be thankful during scarcity. May I learn from my own difficulties how to be a defender of the poor and neglected.

While recovering from sickness

O Lord, you are the Great Healer. Please grant to me your power that can turn my sickness to health and my weakness to strength. Give me a steady recovery, and help me to glorify you during this process.

Fear of death

God of the living, remind me that this earthly life is brief and uncertain. Give me the faith to see in death the gateway to eternal life, so that with a sense of peace I can continue my journey here. Lord Jesus, you took away the sting of death when you died and then rose from the grave, victorious over all darkness and evil. Help me to follow you in faith, that I may meet death unafraid and wake up in your likeness.

When in grief

Grant us courage Lord, at the death of this person we loved, to meet each day with steadfast faith in your goodness. Help us not to sorrow without hope, but in thankful remembrance of a life that touched ours and in expectation of that great reunion when all the dead shall rise, and we will all live forever in your kingdom.